Ongwe oweh oadeh sigwa....deh
weso sigwa neh ga·ya·dos·hah dio·

FULTON PUBLIC LIBRARY
FULTON · NEW YORK

LET'S PLAY

ICE HOCKEY

Shane McFee

PowerKiDS
press.
New York

Published in 2008 by The Rosen Publishing Group, Inc.
29 East 21st Street, New York, NY 10010

First Edition

Editors: Jennifer Way and Nicole Pristash
Book Design: Greg Tucker
Photo Researcher: Nicole Pristash

Photo Credits: Cover © Gemstone Images/Getty Images; pp. 5, 9, 13, 17, 19 Shutterstock.com; p. 7 © Dave Reede/Getty Images; p. 15 © www.istockphoto.com/Michael Braun; pp. 11, 21 © Getty Images.

Library of Congress Cataloging-in-Publication Data

McFee, Shane.
  Let's play ice hockey / by Shane McFee. — 1st ed.
      p. cm. — (Let's get active)
  Includes index.
  ISBN 978-1-4042-4195-4 (library binding)
  1. Hockey—Juvenile literature. I. Title.
  GV847.25.M356 2008
  796.962—dc22
                                        2007034663

Manufactured in the United States of America

Contents

Ice Hockey

Ice hockey is a very fun sport that is played in many countries around the world. It is generally played in places that have cold weather because it is played on ice. Ice hockey is very popular in the United States. It is also Canada's biggest sport.

Ice hockey is a hard sport to learn. It requires a lot of skills. These skills, though, can be learned and practiced. Ice hockey is also a very fast game. This makes it fun to play on a team and to watch!

Ice hockey is a great game to play during the winter months. You can play inside or outside, like this boy.

From Grass to Ice

It is believed that hockey began in northern Europe over 500 years ago. The game was first played on a grassy field. Ice hockey began when the players wanted to play in the winter but could not because their field was covered in snow. Instead of the field, they played on a **frozen** pond or lake.

The first **organized** game of ice hockey was played in Montreal, Canada, in 1875. Students from McGill University made up the rules. Two years later, the rules were printed in the town newspaper. Since then, ice hockey has grown into the sport we play today.

These boys are playing hockey on a frozen pond. Many people play on ponds or lakes when the ice gets thick enough.

Skates and Sticks

You will need gear to play ice hockey. One important thing to have is a pair of ice-hockey skates. Skates are boots that have a metal blade stuck to the bottom. Because ice is **slippery**, the blades slide on the ice and help the player move without falling.

Ice-hockey players hit a puck instead of a ball. A puck is a small disk made of special rubber. You will also need a hockey stick. Hockey sticks are used to hit the puck. The bottom of the stick is curved, or bended, so that it is easier for the puck to rise off the ice when the player hits it.

Ice-hockey pucks are frozen for a few hours before each game. This is to keep the puck from bouncing on the ice when a player hits it.

The Rink

Ice hockey is played in a large, rectangular area called a rink. An ice-hockey rink looks like an indoor soccer field. Instead of grass, though, the floor of the rink is made of ice.

There is a goal net at each end of the rink. The object of the game is to hit the puck into the other team's goal. The players have to skate down the rink and hit the puck into the net. Each goal is worth one point. The team with the most points at the end of the game wins.

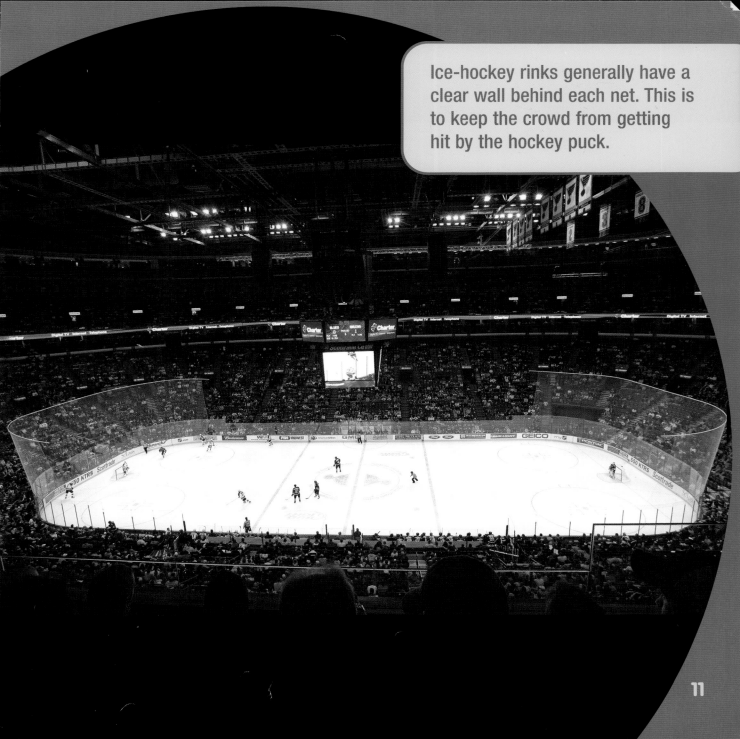

Ice-hockey rinks generally have a clear wall behind each net. This is to keep the crowd from getting hit by the hockey puck.

The Team

Two teams play a game of ice hockey. Each team has six players on the ice. The goalie guards the goal. He has a special stick, which blocks shots. The goalie is the only player who can touch the puck with his hands.

There are three players called forwards. They play **offense**. They are the center, the left wing, and the right wing. The forwards try to score goals by moving the puck closer to the other team's goal. The other two players play **defense**. They try to steal the puck from the forwards on the other team. They also try to keep the puck away from their own goal.

Goalies have many ways of blocking the puck. This goalie is using his glove to catch the puck.

Penalty Box

It is important for ice-hockey players to follow the rules. Every hockey game has a team of **officials**. Officials skate on the ice with the players and make sure that both teams are playing fairly.

If an ice-hockey player breaks the rules, an official will stop the game. The player has to sit in an area called the **penalty** box for at least 2 minutes. This gives the other team an edge. It will have more players on the ice. This is called a power play.

An ice-hockey official must pay close attention during a game. This official is making sure the players are playing the game fairly.

The Coach

Like many sports teams, ice-hockey teams have coaches. The coach is the leader of the team. She is in charge of the team's **strategy**. A strategy is a set of plays used to fool the other team. The coach also decides when to **substitute** players during the game. Players get tired if they are on the ice for a long time. The coach will substitute players with others who have rested.

The coach also leads the team in practice. Ice-hockey players must practice shooting, puck control, and passing. Passing is when one player hits the puck to another player on her team. Goalies practice blocking shots.

Ice-hockey coaches have to make sure every player understands her plays. This coach is drawing a picture of a play on the ice.

Teamwork

Playing ice hockey will teach you many different skills. It will also teach you the value of teamwork. Teamwork is working together for the good of the team. A good ice-hockey player cannot keep the puck to himself. He must pass the puck to his teammates.

Ice hockey will also teach you sportsmanship. Sportsmanship means playing fairly. If you hit a player on the other team with your stick, you will be sent to the penalty box. The other team will then have more players on the ice. This will hurt your team.

The player in the middle is helping the goalie block the puck. He is practicing good teamwork.

Meet Sidney Crosby

Sidney Crosby is one of the youngest players in the National Hockey **League**, or the NHL. The NHL is the highest level of **professional** hockey in North America. Teams from the United States and Canada form the NHL. Crosby is a center for the Pittsburgh Penguins. In 2005, Crosby became the youngest team captain in the history of professional American sports. He was only 19!

Crosby has won many **awards**. He has won the NHL's awards for Most Valuable Player, Leading Scorer, and Outstanding Player. Crosby is already one of the best ice-hockey players in the history of the sport.

In his first five years of playing professional hockey, Sidney Crosby scored more than 70 points!

Let's Get Active!

There are many ways you can start playing ice hockey. Many areas of the United States have ice-hockey teams that you can play on. Ask your parents to help you find a league that you can join.

If you do not live near an ice-hockey rink, you can play outdoor hockey on Rollerblades. Some people call this street hockey. You should never play hockey in the street, though! Maybe you or one of your friends has a big driveway. Driveways are excellent places to play outdoor hockey. Be safe and wear a helmet!

Glossary

awards (uh-WORDZ) Special honors given to someone.

defense (DEE-fents) When a team tries to keep the other team from scoring a goal.

frozen (FROH-zen) Hardened by great cold.

league (LEEG) An organized group.

offense (AH-fents) When a team tries to score points in a game.

officials (uh-FIH-shulz) People who are in charge.

organized (OR-guh-nyzd) To have made rules.

penalty (PEH-nul-tee) A correction for breaking a rule.

professional (pruh-FESH-nul) Someone who is paid for what he or she does.

slippery (SLIH-puh-ree) Hard to hold on to.

strategy (STRA-tuh-jee) Planning and directing sports plays.

substitute (SUB-stuh-toot) To put someone or something in place of another.

Index

Web Sites

Due to the changing nature of Internet links, PowerKids Press has developed an online list of Web sites related to the subject of this book. This site is updated regularly. Please use this link to access the list:
www.powerkidslinks.com/lga/hock/